US ARMY AIR CAVALRY UNIT PATCHES (2001-2025)
COMMEMORATING A LEGACY OF VALOR AND SERVICE TO THE NATION

CW4 DAN McCLINTON (US CAVALRY/RET)

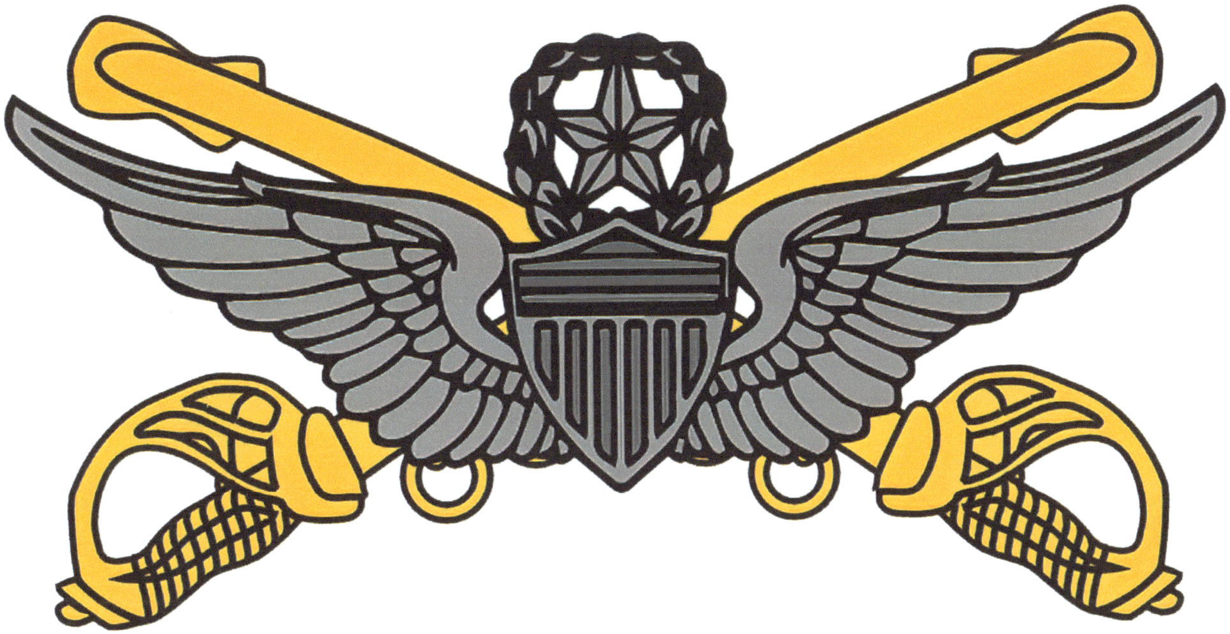

OTHER BOOKS BY THE AUTHOR

MILITARY INSIGNIA

US ARMY AIR CAVALRY PATCHES (2001-2021)
US ARMY ATTACK HELICOPTER UNIT PATCHES (2001-2021)
US ARMY AIR ASSAULT & GENERAL SUPPORT HELICOPTER UNIT PATCHES (2001-2021) VOL 1
US ARMY AIR ASSAULT & GENERAL SUPPORT HELICOPTER UNIT PATCHES (2001-2021) VOL 2
US ARMY ATTACK and AIR CAVALRY UNIT PATCHES (2001-2024)
US ARMY AH-64 PATCHES and INSIGNIA (1975-2025)

PHOTOGRAPHY

37 MONTHS: IMAGES FROM THREE COMBAT TOURS IN IRAQ

MILITARY HISTORY

CRAZYHORSE: FLYING APACHE ATTACK HELICOPTERS WITH THE 1ST CAVALRY DIVISION IN IRAQ (2006-2007)

TABLE OF CONTENTS

INTRODUCTION 4
RED OVER WHITE: A SHORT HISTORY OF THE ORIGIN OF CAVALRY TRADITIONS 5

THE APACHE PATCH 9

ACTIVE DUTY UNITS 10
1ST CAVALRY REGIMENT
2ND CAVALRY REGIMENT
3RD CAVALRY REGIMENT
4TH CAVALRY REGIMENT
6TH CAVALRY REGIMENT
7TH CAVALRY REGIMENT
10TH CAVALRY REGIMENT
17TH CAVALRY REGIMENT

NATIONAL GUARD AND RESERVE UNITS 106
7TH SQUADRON 6TH CAVALRY REGIMENT (US ARMY RESERVE)
C COMPANY 1ST BATTALION 185TH AVIATION REGIMENT (MISSISSIPPI ARMY NATIONAL GUARD)
1ST SQUADRON 230TH ARMORED CAVALRY REGIMENT (TENNESSEE ARMY NATIONAL GUARD)
4TH SQUADRON 278TH ARMORED CAVALRY REGIMENT (TENNESSEE ARMY NATIONAL GUARD)

US ARMY AVIATION CENTER of EXCELLENCE (FORT RUCKER / NOVOSEL) 115

21ST CAVALRY BRIGADE (AKA APACHE TRAINING BRIGADE) 122

AIRCRAFT and GENERIC PATCHES 123

ACKNOWLEDGMENTS 126

INTRODUCTION

Welcome to this sixth in a series of books featuring the patches and insignia of aviation units serving in the United States Army. As you may has deduced by the title, this volume will feature the insignia that were used by US Army Air Cavalry helicopter units during the time period starting at September 11, 2001 until the year 2025. Unfortunately, at this time it appears that the US Army is divesting itself of all Air Cavalry units and at least on the Army aviation side of things, almost all things "cavalry" will soon be a thing of the past. If you are a new reader of these books, thank you for buying this one and I hope you enjoy it. If you are a returning reader, I appreciate your continued support and hope that this book fulfills your expectations!

For those that are unfamiliar with the structure and organization of modern Army Aviation a quick history lesson might be in order. The birth of modern Army Aviation occurred during the Vietnam War when helicopters began to be used in battle in large numbers. During that conflict the first purpose-built Attack Helicopter (AH-1 Cobra) saw service in Air Cavalry Troops, Attack Helicopter Companies, and Aerial Rocket Artillery units. When the Vietnam War ended and the focus was changed towards the Cold War and possible conflict with the Soviet Union the use of the armed helicopter as a anti-armor weapon was begun. With that came the formation of Attack Helicopter Battalions and the development of what was to become the AH-64 Apache attack helicopter. The birth of the Army Aviation branch in 1983 saw further organization and formation of the Aviation regimental system to identify units and codify their historical lineage which is still in use today.

During the time period covered in this book Scout and Attack helicopters were fielded and deployed to combat in Attack Helicopter Battalions, Cavalry troops, squadrons and Regiments and later in Attack Reconnaissance Battalions. Units are organized in this book by their regimental designation. I did this in part because there has been a lot of shifting and moving of units over the last 24 years and this made the most sense to me. I apologize in advance if this causes any confusion for the reader. Additionally, I have identified locations by historical names. In 2023 the Department of Defense renamed several Army installations to remove the names of former members of the Confederacy that were used to identify several US Army posts. In the interest on completeness and historical accuracy I have retained the old names and have added the new names where appropriate. This is not meant as a protest or statement about the process, it is just an attempt to maintain a complete and accurate record.

On September 11, 2001 the US Army was in a state of transition to what at the time was referred to as "digital warfighting". A major portion of that transition consisted of the divestiture of legacy weapons systems such as the AH-64A and moving towards systems with built in digital architecture such as the AH-64D Longbow Apache. It also saw "light" units such as the 10th Mountain and 25th Infantry Division aviation brigade's attack helicopter battalions fielded with the OH-58 Kiowa Warrior helicopter. Initially intended as a stop-gap solution to fill the need for a smaller scout aircraft with a limited ability to conduct offensive operations until the RAH-66 Comanche could be fielded, the Kiowa Warrior ended up serving in attack roles until replaced around 2006 and in the Cavalry role (after the cancellation of the RAH-66) until the aircraft was retired from the inventory in 2016.

Currently all US Army Air Cavalry units operate a combination of the AH-64D, AH-64E along with various Unmanned Aerial Systems (UAS). The AH-64E is expected to eventually replace all AH-64Ds around 2027 and serve in the fleet until at least the year 2040. At the time of publication, all Air Cavalry units are slated to be closed down by the end of FY 26. This is a sad end for units that have a great legacy of service, honor and valor. I hope this volume serves in some way to help preserve the legacy that was forged in blood by the Air Cavalry across the globe. As a former cavalryman, it will be a sad day indeed when the last guidon is struck down. We will always remember, till Fiddler's Green.

Air Cav!

CW4 DAN McCLINTON (US CAVALRY, RETIRED)

RED OVER WHITE: a short history of the AIR CAVALRY and its traditions

The cavalry has a long and storied history in the United States Army. On the 12th of December 1776, the Congress formed the first Cavalry unit in the United States Army. In 1834 Army General regulations authorized a red over white guidon for companies of dragoons (cavalry). It was to be made of silk and its dimensions were to be 27 X 41 inches with a 15-inch swallowtail. The letters US in white were located on the upper red portion and the troop letter would be sewn in red on the lower white portion. In 1862 General Order 4 (dated January 18) stated that "Guidons and camp colors will be made like the United States flag with stars and stripes."

The typical design had the stars in two concentric circles with one star in each corner of the canton. The dimensions remained as in 1834. Over the course of the Civil War, it became customary to paint the stars in gold instead of silver (which tarnished). In 1885 General Order 10 returned the guidon colors to the 1834 standard. With some changes in dimensions, materials and letter placement the cavalry guidon has remained red and white ever since. As such, these colors are associated with the cavalry and used everywhere to include patches.

"Cavalry and I don't mean horses" THE GENESIS OF THE AIR CAV

In the late 50's and early 60's there was a group of people within the Army that began to champion the concept of what was called at that time "Sky Cav". This led to several experiments that culminated with the formation of the first Aerial Reconnaissance and Security Troop. On 24 September 1962 D Troop (Air) 17th Cavalry was formed at Fort Rucker, AL. Later, in 1963 it would become B Troop 3rd Squadron 17th Cavalry when 3/17 CAV was activated at FT Benning, GA.

In 1962, as a part of what was called the Reorganization Objective Army Division (ROAD), an air cavalry troop was to be established in each division. ROAD led to the establishment of D TRP (Air) 4/12 CAV at FT Carson and D TRP (Air) 2/15 CAV in Germany as a part of 4AD which was re designated D TRP 2/4 CAV in August 1963.

During the testing and train-up of the 11th Air Assault Division for deployment to Vietnam 3/17 CAV lived in the field and proved the concept of the air cavalry. On 15 November 1964 the 11th Air Assault Division was re-designated the 1st Cavalry Division (Airmoble) and 3/17 CAV was re-designated 1/9 CAV. They were deployed to Vietnam ninety days later. During the Vietnam War fifteen different Air Cavalry units saw combat. On 26 February 1973 seven air cavalry troops became the last US combat elements to depart Vietnam.

AIR CAV POST-VIETNAM

At the close of the Vietnam War the Army's attention returned to primarily Europe and the threat posed by the Warsaw Pact forces led by the Soviet Union. Divisional cavalry squadrons were equipped with two troops of OH-58 scout helicopters and AH-1 Cobra attack helicopters to perform their missions. Likewise at the Corps level Armored Cavalry Regiments were also equipped with aviation assets to carry out their missions. In the mid 80s with the arrival of the concept of Air-Land Battle and the AH-64 Apache, things began to change. The concept of "deep attack" was developed to help counter the Soviets numerical advantage in armor. To facilitate this doctrine, the 6th Air Cavalry Brigade (Air Combat) and 11th Attack Helicopter Regiment were formed. The AH-64 began replacing the venerable AH-1 in attack battalions and some armored cavalry regiments like 11th ACR in Germany. The 1st, 2nd, 3rd, 4th, 5th, and 6th Regiments of the 6th Cavalry were formed and fielded with the AH-64. Divisional cavalry squadrons continued to soldier on with a mix of OH-58C and AH-1 aircraft until the mid 1990's when both aircraft were replaced with OH-58D Kiowa Warriors. It was around that same time period when air cavalry squadrons that had AH-64s lost their UH-60s and OH-58 aircraft and became pure AH-64 units. This would be the makeup of US Army air cavalry units on September 11, 2001.

AIR CAV and the GLOBAL WAR on TERROR

When the US Army first entered battle after the events of 9/11 it was task organized much as it had been since the mid 1990's. But after the invasion of Iraq in 2003 the aviation assets of Cavalry units were stripped out and assigned to aviation task forces that supported ground units on an as needed basis. In 2007 during the first of many reorganizations to come the aviation assets (by this time OH-58D Kiowa Warriors) of the Divisional Cavalry Squadrons were stripped away and the separate air cavalry squadrons/attack battalions at the Corps level (2nd and 3rd ACR, 6th Cavalry BDE (Korea) and 11th Attack Regiment (Germany)) were eliminated. At the same time, heavy divisions (1CD, 1AD, 1ID, 2ID, 3ID, 4ID) fielded two Attack Reconnaissance Battalions (ARB) (AH-64D) and Light Divisions (10th MTN, 25 ID, 82 ABN) had an attack battalion and cavalry squadron both equipped with the OH-58D Kiowa Warrior. The 101st Air Assault Division was unique in that it contained the most aviation assets in the US Army and had at one time three attack battalions fielding the AH-64 and a air cavalry squadron that operated the OH-58D. In 2014 the decision was made to retire the OH-58D Kiowa Warrior. Efforts to develop a dedicated scout platform were unsuccessful and the AH-64 and UAS

Around 2015 in another round of reorganization/renaming, the second ARB in each division was re-flagged as a air cavalry squadron and the remaining ARBs were now called just attack battalions. Additionally the 101st AASSLT Division had its attack helicopter assets reduced to a single attack helicopter battalion. With this action every division in the Army now had one attack helicopter battalion and one air cavalry squadron. This was the organization of assets until 2025.

THE END OF THE AIR CAV?

In early 2025 the US Army announced that it was enacting a policy designed to take advantage of new technologies and incorporate lessons learned from recent conflicts around the world. As a part of this new policy all Air Cavalry Squadrons are to be disbanded by the end of 2026 and the AH-64D will be removed from the inventory, leaving a pure AH-64E fleet. This is a rather ignominious ending to a segment of Army Aviation that has such a distinguished history. There is always hope that at some future date these units and their heritage will be returned to the active Army, but as long as we remember there will always be an AIR CAV.

CAVALRY TRADITIONS

What's with the hat and spurs?

Even though this a book about patches and insignia, no book about the cavalry would be complete without something about the hat or as many refer to it, the Stetson. The first use of the Stetson in the modern army can be traced to LTC Stockton who was the commander of 3/17 CAV at FT Benning, GA. In an effort to increase morale of his troops LTC Stockton authorized the wear of a hat that was manufactured by the Stetson Hat Company and resembled the 1876 campaign hat worn by cavalry troopers of that time period. As the Vietnam War continued virtually all air cavalry units adopted the use of the Stetson, these eventually even spread to ground units. Most hats were black in color with a hat cord that was yellow for enlisted troops, silver with back for warrant officers and gold and black for commissioned officers. Some units had variations as D TRP 3//5 CAV wore gray hats instead of the traditional black ones. This continued when the unit was re-designated C TRP 3/17 CAV (at least it did for a short time).

Wearing of the hat was not mandatory but peer pressure saw almost universal adoption. Additionally, many units held a "wetting down" ceremony where the new hat owner broke in their Stetson by drinking a hat full of beer (or other liquids) from it. The wearing of the hat lives on today, although like many things in the Army the tradition has been gradually watered down or in some places discouraged entirely.

Obviously spurs were originally worn when the cavalry rode horses, but today earning your spurs is a way of showing that you have earned your right to be a part of a cavalry unit. Silver spurs are earned through a process known as a spur ride, where the candidate is required to show that they are worthy by completing various tasks and showing knowledge of cavalry lore. Gold spurs are earned by serving with a cavalry unit in combat.

REFERENCES

If the reader would like to learn more about the history and traditions of the Air Cavalry a good place to start is the book Winged Sabers by Lawrence H Johnson III. It covers the beginnings of the AIR CAV and has a great selection of Vietnam era cavalry images and information.

B TRP 3-6 CAV w/ Standard CAV guidon
(Photo by author)

FIDDLER'S GREEN

Fiddler's Green is a legendary imagined afterlife, where there is perpetual mirth, a fiddle that never stops playing, and dancers who never tire. Its origins are obscure, although some point to the Greek myth of the "Elysian Fields" as a potential inspiration.

Many believe that the origin and author of Fiddler's Green may have originated by the 5th Royal Irish Lancers who trace their origin back to 1689 when a cavalry formation known as Wynne's Regiment of Enniskillen Dragoons was formed by the then governor James Wynne. Although there no evidence that the Irish Lancers appropriated the paradise and incorporated it into a poem that emigrated to the US with its members, or whether the paradise and poem are of US origin.

The cavalry paradise reference seems to be associated with the 7th US Cavalry from the post Civil War era and the Indian Wars period (circa 1860-1870). Now, there is a link between the 7th US Cavalry and Ireland. Many Troopers of the 7th Cavalry were of Irish origin, and the 7th Cavalry's own insignia has the phrase "Garryowen" on it. "Garryowen" is a derivative of the Irish Gaelic Garraí Eóin which means Owen's Garden. Owen's Garden was a commons (open field) in Limerick, Ireland that gave rise to a drinking ballad of the same name. The 5th Royal Irish Lances, an Irish cavalry unit, used that drinking ballad.

The story of Fiddler's Green was first published in the 1923 volume of the Cavalry Journal. According to this article, it was inspired by a story told by Captain "Sammy" Pearson at a campfire in the Medicine Bow Mountains of Wyoming. Common usage also seems to hold this view. As included in John Connally's song from circa 1960 and the Stereophonic's (Welsh Band) song from late 1990's. Fiddler's Green is listed sometimes as a poem and other times as a cavalry prayer. It is still used by modern cavalry units to memorialize the deceased.

Halfway down the trail to Hell,
In a shady meadow green
Are the Souls of all dead Troopers camped,
Near a good old-time canteen.
And this eternal resting place
Is known as Fiddlers' Green.

Marching past, straight through to Hell
The Infantry are seen.
Accompanied by the Engineers,
Artillery and Marines,
For none but the shades of Cavalrymen
Dismount at Fiddlers' Green.

Though some go curving down the trail
To seek a warmer scene.
No Trooper ever gets to Hell
Ere he's emptied his canteen.
And so rides back to drink again
With friends at Fiddlers' Green.

And so when man and horse go down
Beneath a saber keen,
Or in a roaring charge of fierce melee
You stop a bullet clean,
And the hostiles come to get your scalp,
Just empty your canteen,
And put your pistol to your head
And go to Fiddlers' Green.

THE APACHE PATCH: I See A Pattern Here

To even the most casual observer it is fairly obvious that most of the patches that have been or are being used in units that are equipped with versions of the AH-64 Apache have a definite theme. While there is no authority or regulation that governs the production, appearance or even wearing of company, troop, battalion or squadron level patches for US Army Aviation there is an undeniable feeling of tradition and a strong push to remember those who came before.

When the AH-64 was named after the Native American Apache tribe in 1981, the art department of the Hughes Helicopter Company also unveiled its logo for the new aircraft (see photo bottom left) and the rest was history. When the aircraft began to be delivered to line units in the mid 80's virtually all unit patches/insignia were based on the original Apache program patch. This tradition has continued (as one can plainly see by the patch designs displayed in this book) to this day. There is symbolism contained in many of these designs. If you look at the original Apache program patch there are 6 stars in the border of the patch, many say this is to recognize that the 6th Air Cavalry Brigade was the first unit to field the Apache. Interestingly enough the 6th US Cavalry was the unit that hunted down and captured the Apache Indian leader Geronimo during the Indian Wars of the mid to late 1800's. Other patch designs have featured 10 stars which represent the original 10 divisional attack battalions. As anyone familiar with US Army Aviation patches can readily attest there is often no rhyme or reason as to why patches contain the things that they do, or the reasons are only known to those that designed and procured them. Regardless, we appreciate them all....AIR CAV, ATTACK!

ACTIVE DUTY UNITS

An OH-58D Kiowa Warrior from E TRP 1-7 CAV at Camp Taji, Iraq (2004 photo by author)

1st CAVALRY REGIMENT "Courageous and Faithful"
Established 1833

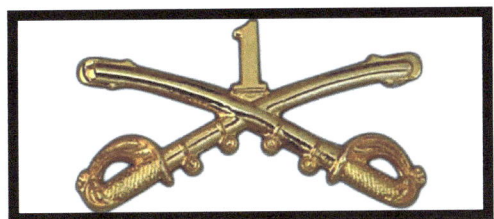

1st SQUADRON 1st CAVALRY REGIMENT
1st Armored Divsion, Katterbach Germany (OH-58D) OIF (Aviation elements reassigned in 2005)

Squadron Patch

D Troop 1-1 CAV "DESPERADO"

E Troop 1-1 CAV "EXCALIBUR"   HHT 1-1 CAV "HEADHUNTERS"

2nd Armored Cavalry Regiment (2nd ACR) "ALWAYS READY"
Established 1836

4th Squadron 2nd Armored Cavalry Regiment "REDCATCHERS"

2nd ACR Fort Polk, LA (OH-58D, UH-60) (Aviation assets reassigned in 2005)

Squadron Patches

N Troop 4-2 ACR "NOMAD" / "THUG" / "NIGHT THUG"

O Troop 4-2 ACR "OUTLAW" / "BLACK DEATH"

P Troop 4-2 ACR "PALEHORSE"

Q Troop 4-2 ACR "QUICKSTRIKE"

R Troop 4-2 ACR "RAPTORS" / "RENEGADE"

S Troop 4-2 ACR "SAVAGE"

Armament Platoon 4-2 ACR "DAWG POUND"

3rd Armored Cavalry Regiment (3rd ACR) "BRAVE RIFLES"
Established 1846

4th Squadron 3rd Cavalry Regiment "LONGKNIFE"
3rd Armored Cavalry Regiment, Fort Bliss, TX

Squadron Patches

N Troop 4-3 ACR "NOMADS"

O Troop 4-3 ACR "OUTLAW"

P Troop 4-3 ACR "PEGASUS"

Q Troop 4-3 ACR "QUICKSILVER"

R Troop 4-3 ACR "RENEGADE"

S Troop 4-3 ACR "STETSON"

T Troop 4-3 ACR "TOMAHAWK"

HHT 4-3 ACR "HEADHUNTERS"

4th Cavalry Regiment "PREPARED and LOYAL"
Established 1855

1st Squadron 4th Cavalry Regiment "QUARTERHORSE"

1st Infantry Division, (OH-58D) OIF: 2004-05

1-4 CAV Squadron patch

HHT 1-4 CAV "WORKHORSE"

D Troop 1-4 CAV "DARKHORSE"

E Troop 1-4 CAV "EAGLE"

F Troop 1-4 CAV "WITCHDOCTORS"

3rd Squadron 4th Cavalry Regiment
25th Infantry Division, (OH-58D) OEF V

B Troop 3-4 CAV "WARLORDS"

C Troop 3-4 CAV "CRAZYHORSE"

6th Cavalry Regiment "FIGHTING SIXTH"
Established 1861

6th AIR CAVALRY BRIGADE "BLACKHORSE"
Camp Humphries, Korea (2001-2005) (AH-64A/D)

1st Squadron 6th Cavalry Regiment "FIGHTING SIXTH"

6th Cavalry Brigade, Camp Eagle, Korea (AH-64 A/D) 1st Infantry Division, Fort Riley, KS (OH-58D /AH-64D)

Squadron Patches

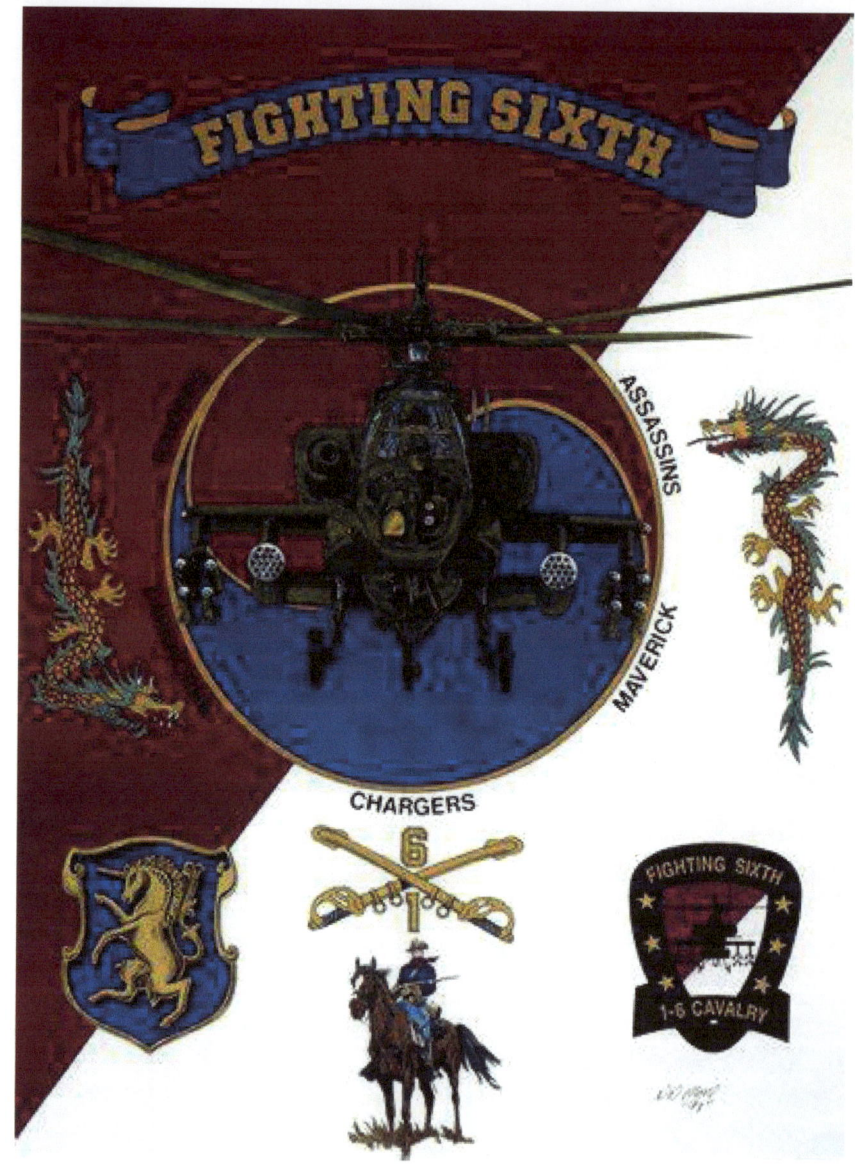

A Troop 1-6 CAV "ASSASSIN / AVENGERS"

B Troop 1-6 CAV "MAVERICKS / BANDITS"

  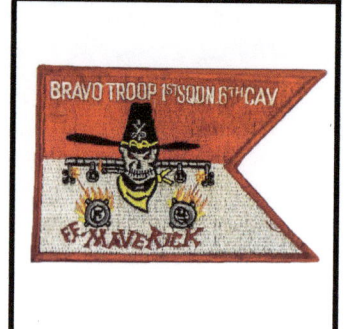  

C Troop 1-6 CAV "BLACKJACK / CRUSADERS"

C Troop continued...

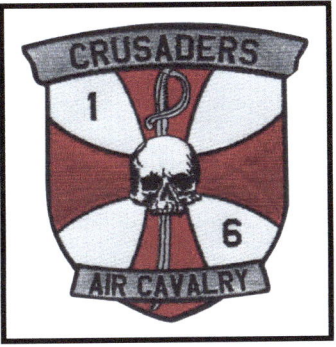    

D Troop 1-6 CAV "DARK ANGELS"

E Troop 1-6 CAV "IRON HORSE"

F Troop 1-6 CAV "FORSAKEN"

HHT 1-6 CAV "SIX SHOOTERS"

2nd Squadron 6th Cavalry Regiment "Real Cav" "Fighting Sixth"

11th AVN REGT (AH-64) OIF 2003, OEF 2006 25th Infantry Division (OH-58D/AH-64) OIF 06-08, 09-10, OEF 12-13

2-6 CAV Squadron Patches

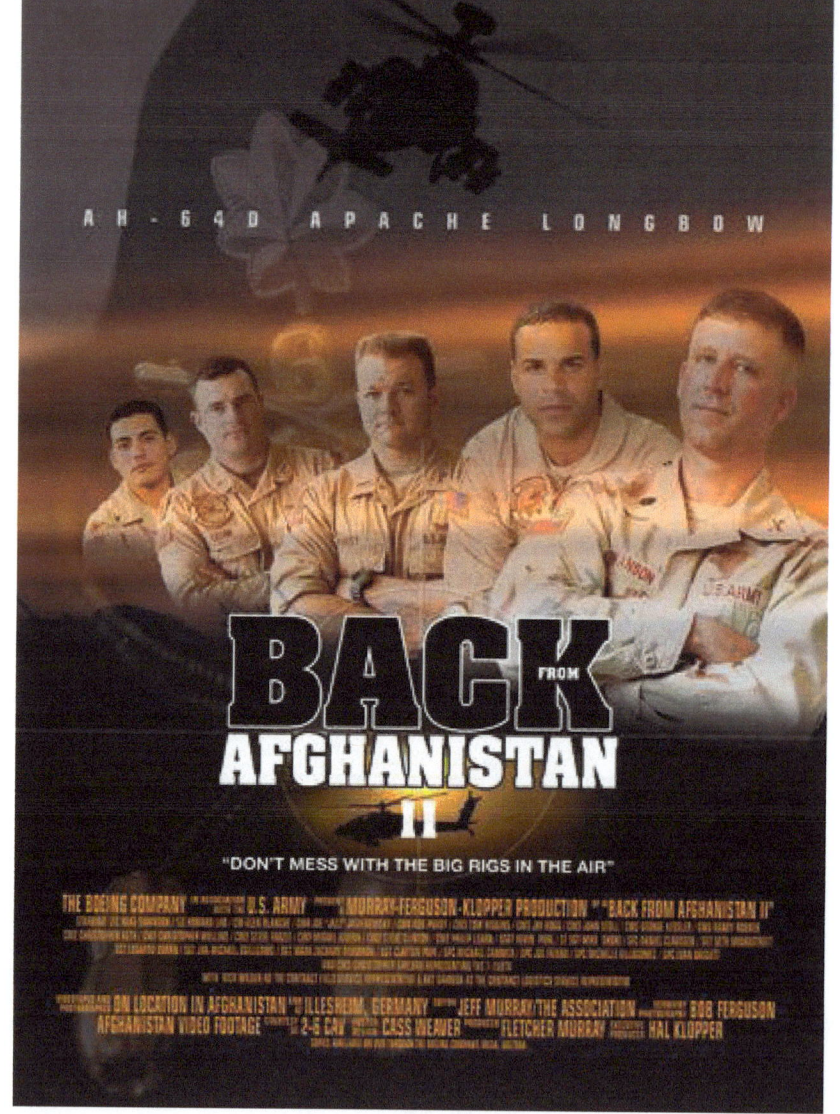

A Troop 2-6 CAV "BLACKJACK" (AH-64, Germany) / "RENEGADES" (OH-58D, AH-64, Hawaii)

 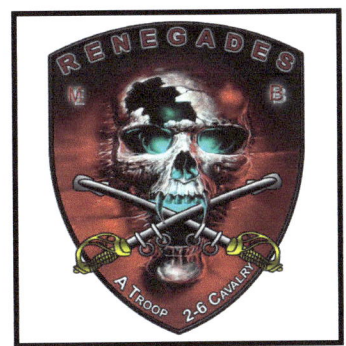  

A Troop continued...

B Troop 2-6 CAV "SHOCK TROOP" (AH-64, Germany) / "GHOSTRIDER" (OH-58D. AH-64, Hawaii) / "SHOCK TROOP" (AH-64, Hawaii)

B Troop continued ...

C Troop 2-6 CAV "PHANTOMS / CHAOS"

   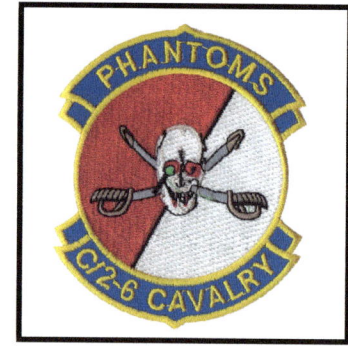 

C Troop continued...

D Troop 2-6 CAV "OUTLAWS" / "DESPERADOS" / "OUTLAWS"

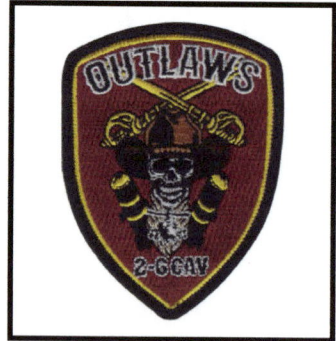
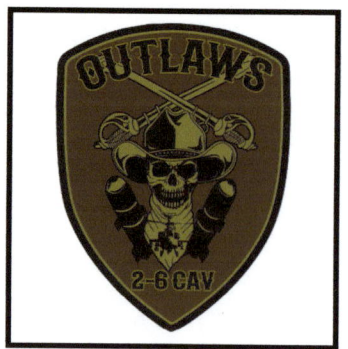

E Troop 2-6 CAV "LONGHORNS" / "EXECUTIONERS"

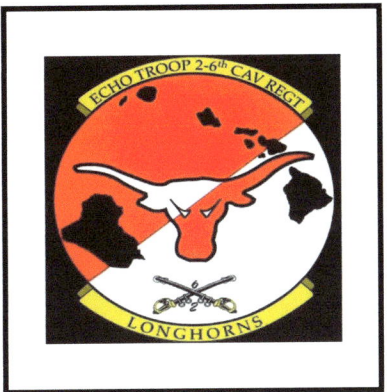

HHT 2-6 CAV "HELLHORSE" / "STETSONS"

3rd Squadron 6th Cavalry Regiment "HEAVY CAV"

6th Air Cavalry Brigade, Camp Humpries, Korea (AH-64 A/D) 1st Armored Division, Fort Bliss, TX (AH-64D/E)

Squadron and Task Force and Morale Patches

 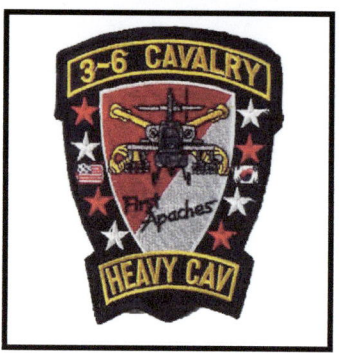  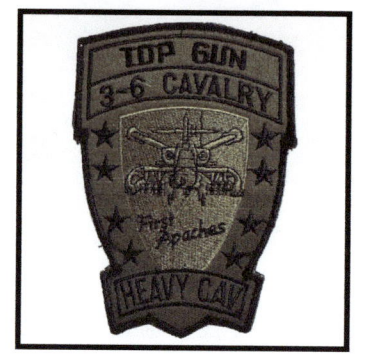 

3-6 CAVALRY
HEAVY CAV

3-6 CAVALRY
HEAVY CAV

TASK FORCE HEAVY CAV
OFS
2019
JALALABAD

DEPLORABLE

HIT MY SPOT

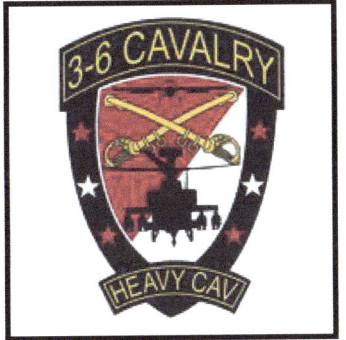

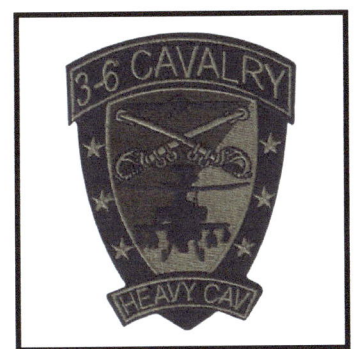

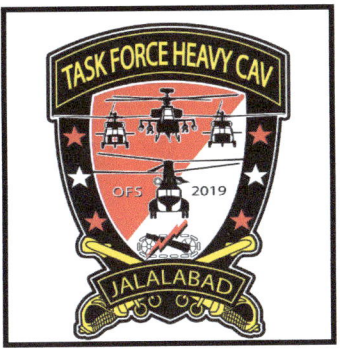

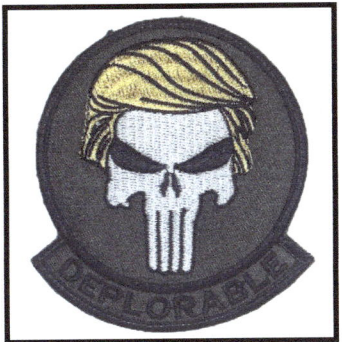

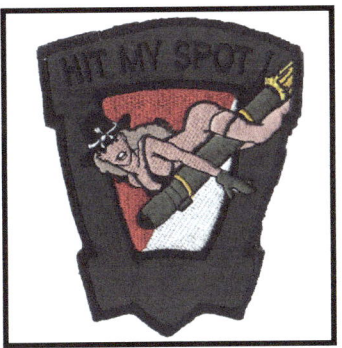

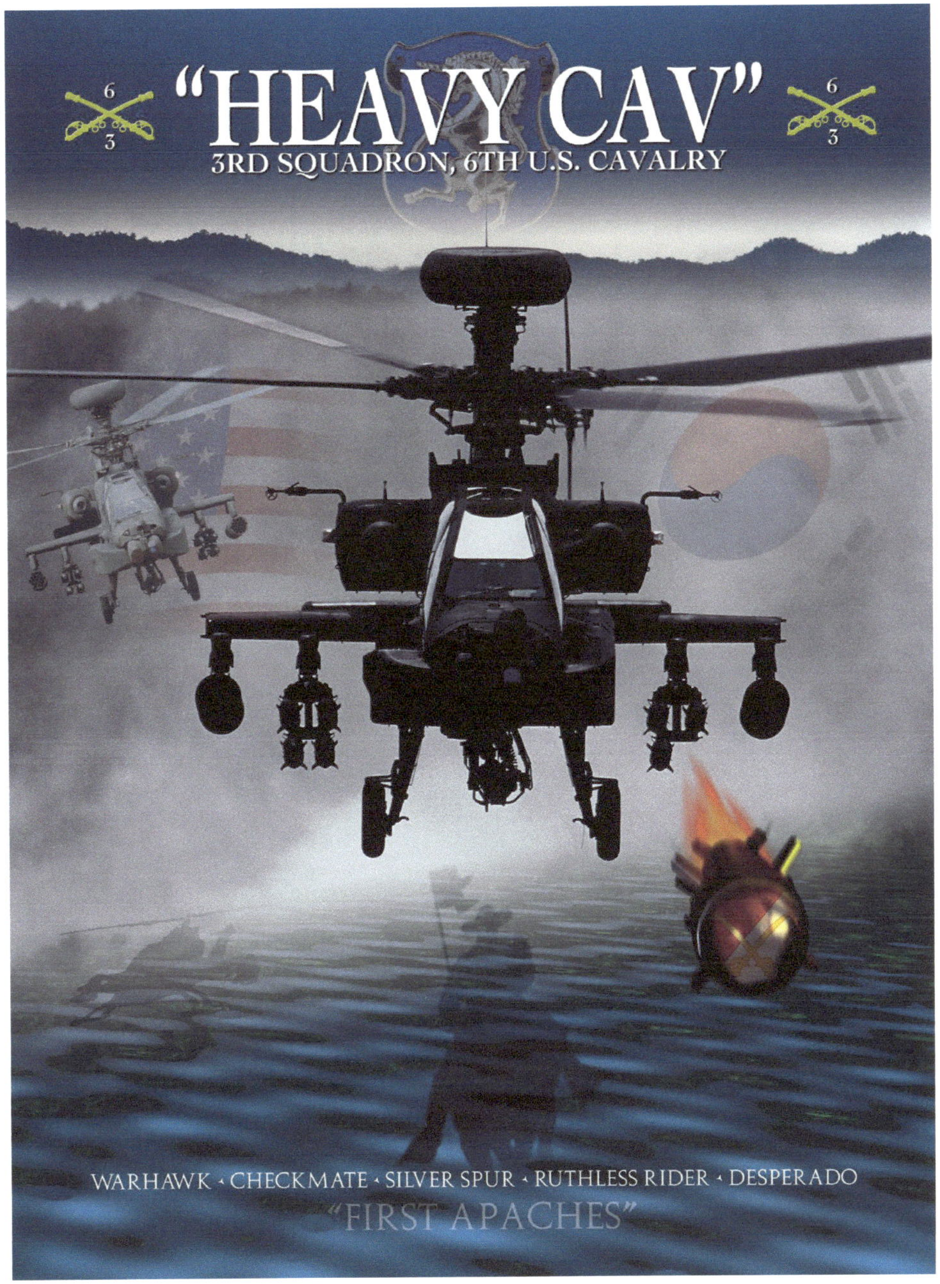

"HEAVY CAV"
3RD SQUADRON, 6TH U.S. CAVALRY
WARHAWK · CHECKMATE · SILVER SPUR · RUTHLESS RIDER · DESPERADO
"FIRST APACHES"

A Troop 3-6 CAV "CHECKMATES"

B Troop 3-6 CAV "SILVER SPUR"

C Troop 3-6 CAV "RUTHLESS RIDERS"

D Troop 3-6 CAV "DESPERADO"

E Troop 3-6 CAV "OUTLAWS"

HHT 3-6 CAV "WARHAWKS"

4th Squadron 6th Cavalry "REDCATCHERS"

FT Lewis, WA (OH-58D) OIF 07-09 (AH-64) OIR 16-17

4-6 CAV Squadron Patches

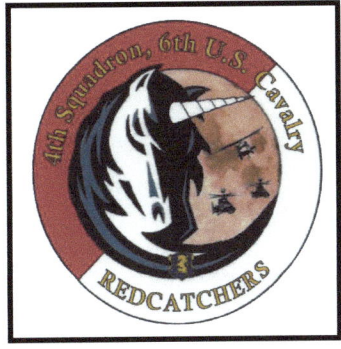  

NIGHT RIDERS
4th Squadron
6th Cavalry
AH-64 APACHE
FIRST ACTIVATING APACHE SQUADRON

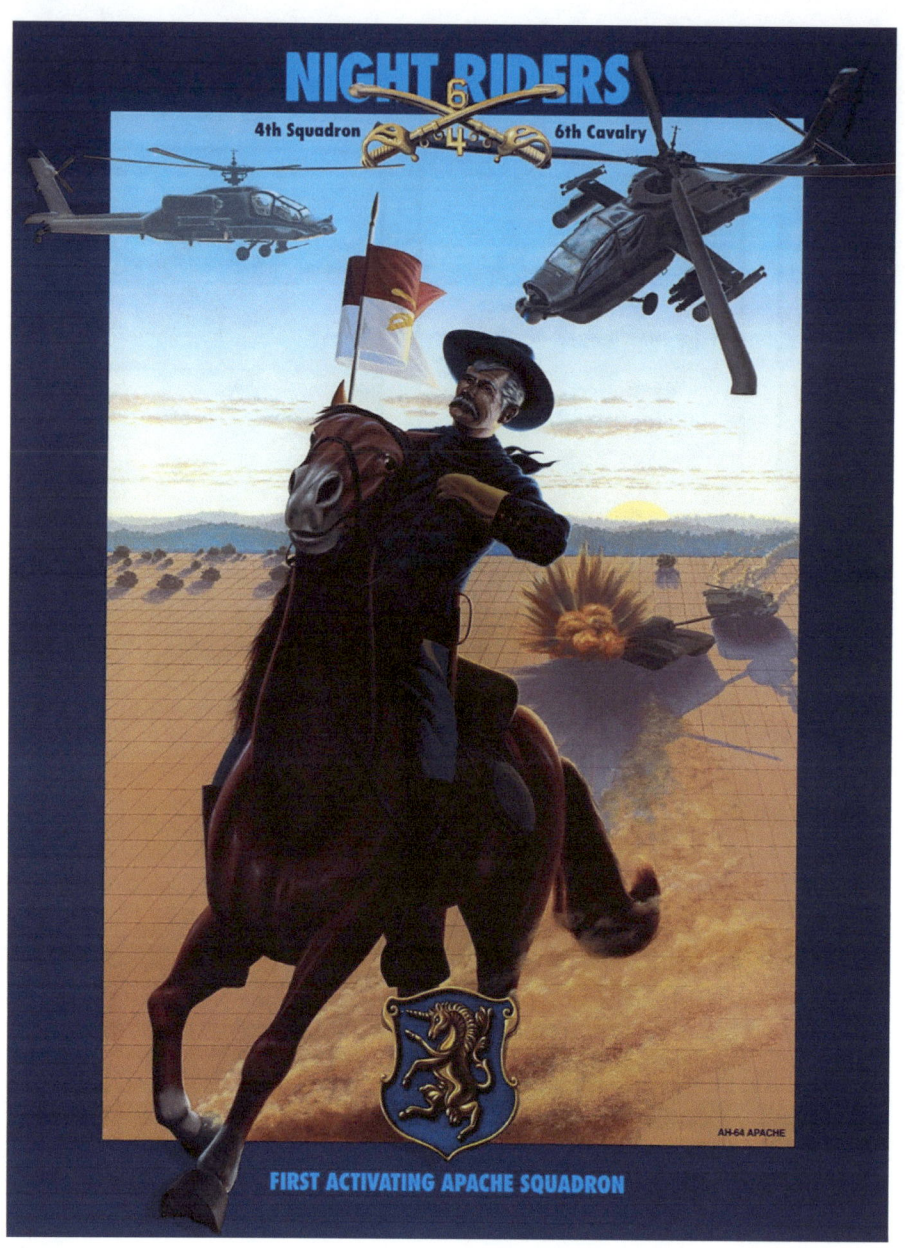

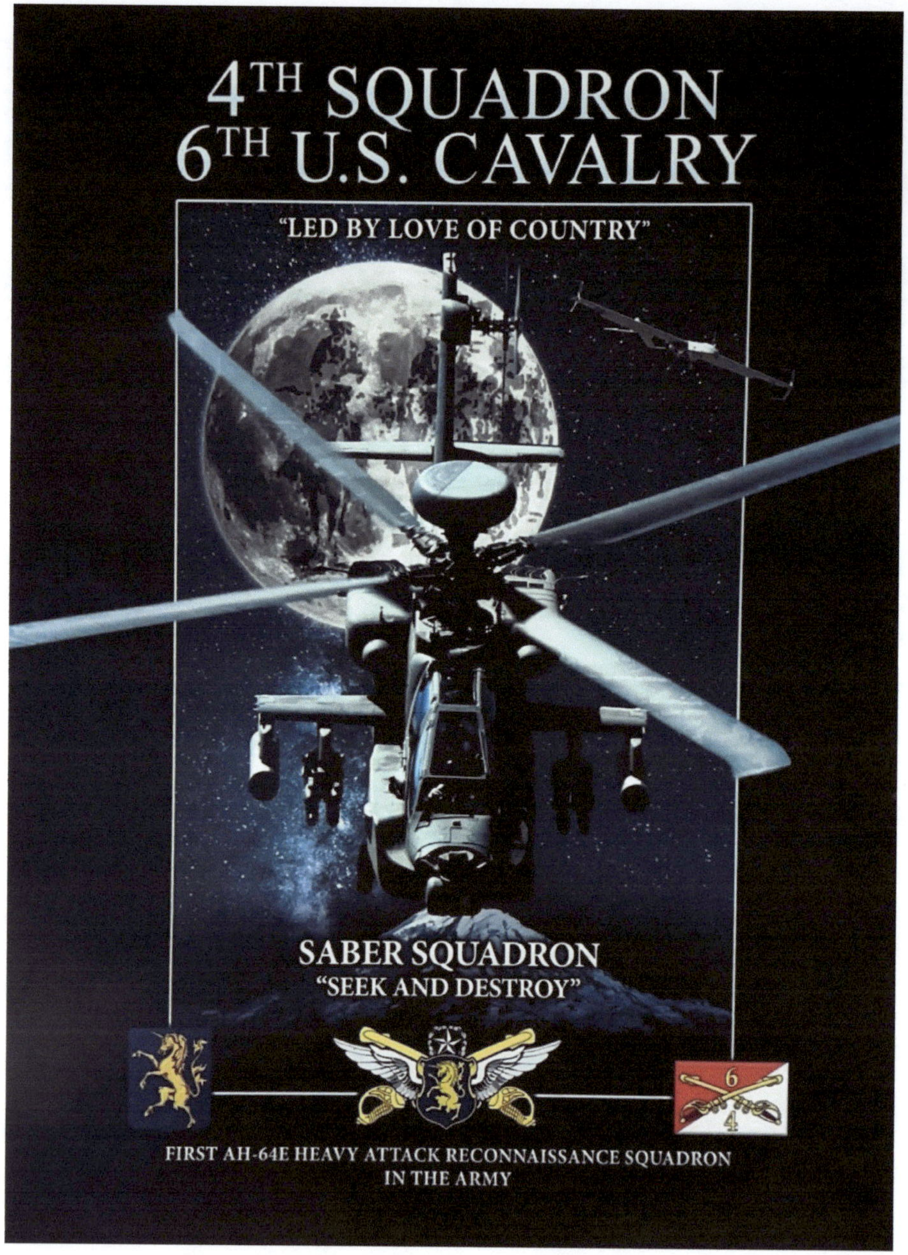
4TH SQUADRON
6TH U.S. CAVALRY
"LED BY LOVE OF COUNTRY"
SABER SQUADRON
"SEEK AND DESTROY"
FIRST AH-64E HEAVY ATTACK RECONNAISSANCE SQUADRON
IN THE ARMY

A Troop 4-6 CAV "THUGS" / "ACES" / "RAZORBACKS"

B Troop 4-6 CAV "BLACK DEATH"

C Troop 4-6 CAV "CARNAGE"

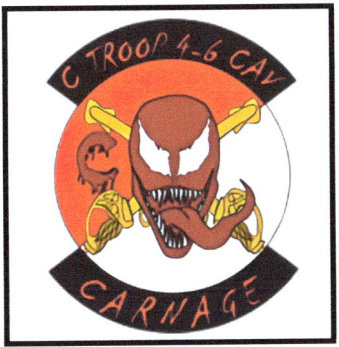

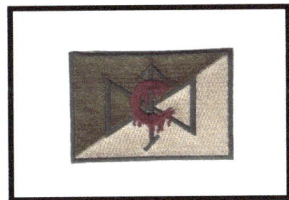

D Troop 4-6 CAV "DARK HORSE"

E Troop 4-6 CAV "EXECUTIONER" / "EASY RIDER" / "ROUGH RIDER"

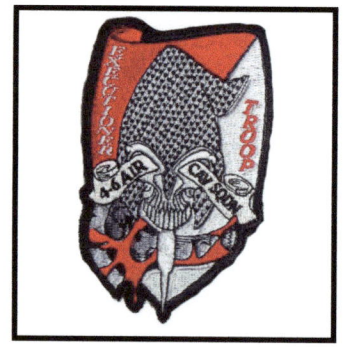

F Troop 4-6 CAV "FIRE HORSE"

G Troop 4-6 CAV "GHOST RIDERS"

HHT 4-6 CAV "WORKHORSE" / "ARCHANGELS" / "HEADHUNTERS"

6th Squadron 6th Cavalry "SIX SHOOTERS"

11th AVN Regiment, Illesheim, Germany (AH-64) OIF 10th MTN DIV, FT Drum, NY (OH-58D / AH-64D) OEF, OFS

6-6 CAV Squadron Patches

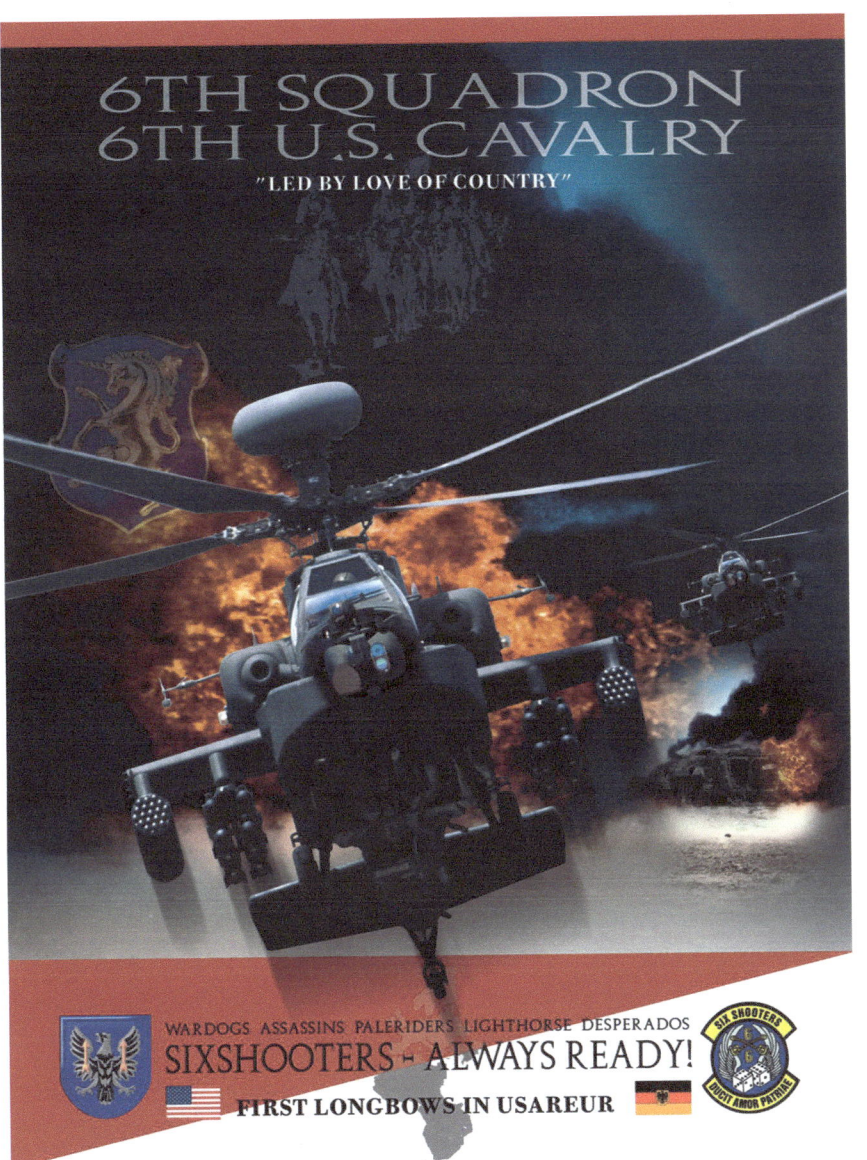
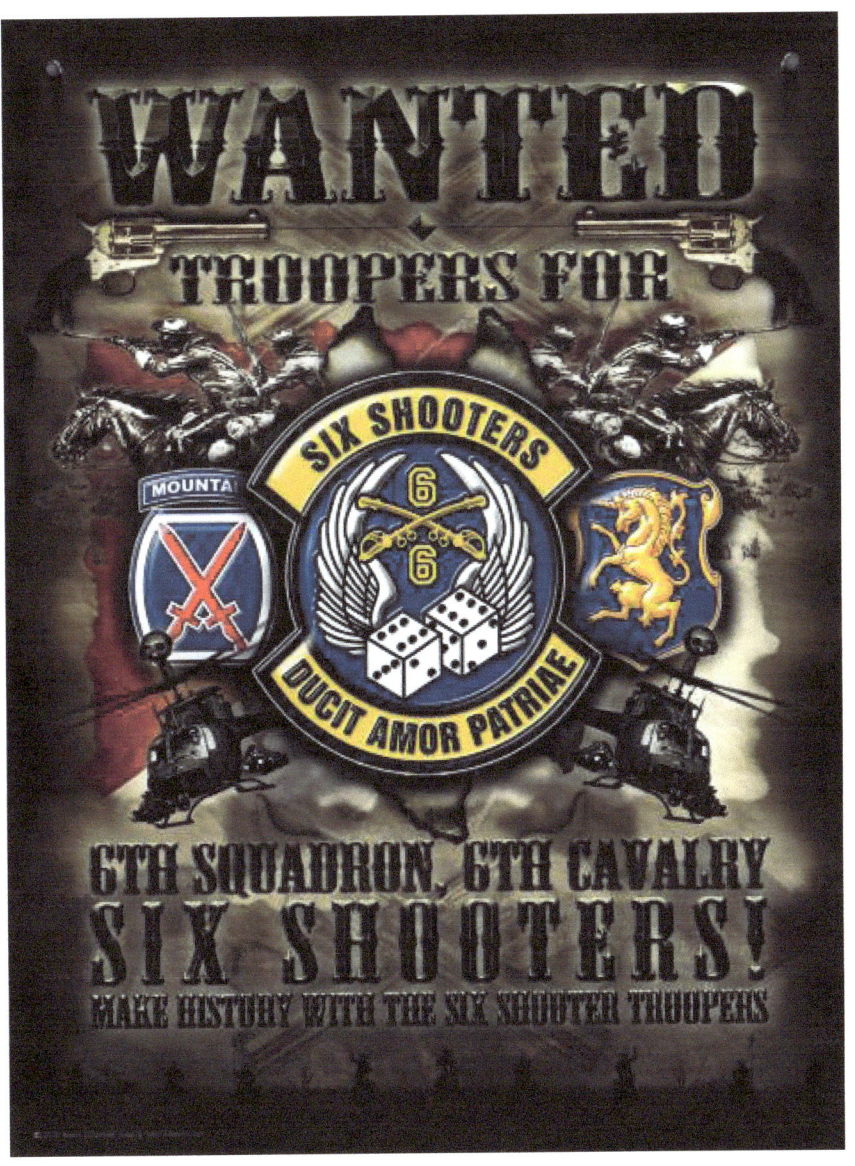

A Troop 6-6 CAV "ASSASSINS"

B Troop 6-6 CAV "PALERIDERS"

C Troop 6-6 CAV "OUTCASTS"

   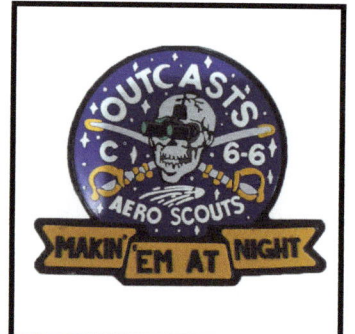 

D Troop 6-6 CAV "DESPERADOS"

E Troop 6-6 CAV "MUSTANGS" / "GHOST RIDERS"   **HHT 6-6 CAV "HELLRAISERS"**

7th CAVALRY REGIMENT
Established 1866

1st Squadron 7th Cavalry Regiment "GARRYOWEN"

1st Cavlary Division, Fort Hood, TX (OH-58D) OIF 2 (Aviation assets reassigned in 2005)

 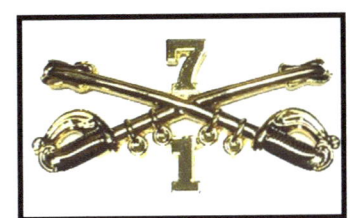

 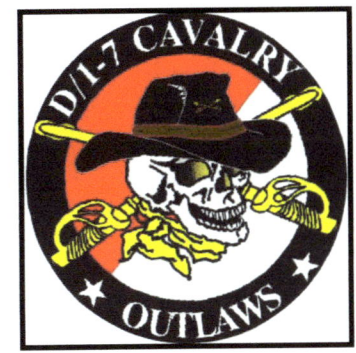   

3rd Squadron 7th Cavalry Regiment

3rd Infantry Division, Fort Stewart, Georgia (OH-58D) OIF

Squadron Patch

| D Troop 3-7 CAV "DEMON" | E Troop 3-7 CAV "EAGLE" | HHT 3-7 CAV "HAVOC" |

4th Squadron 7th Cavalry Regiment
2nd Infantry Division, Camp Stanton, Korea (OH-58D)

D Troop 4-7 CAV "DAGGER"

E Troop 4-7 CAV "HORSEMEN"

Korean made patches for D, E, and F Troops

10th Cavalry Regiment "READY AND FORWARD"
Established 1866

1st Squadron 10th Cavalry

4th Infantry Division, FT Hood, TX (OH-58D) OIF

D Troop 1-10 CAV "DRAGOONS"

E Troop 1-10 CAV "EASY"

17th Cavalry Regiment "FORWARD"
Established 1916

1st Squadron 17th Cavalry "PALEHORSE"

82nd Airborne Division, Fort Bragg/Liberty, NC (OH-58D/AH-64) OIF3, OIF 06-08, OEF 09-10, OEF 11-12, OEF 14

1-17th CAV Squadron Patches

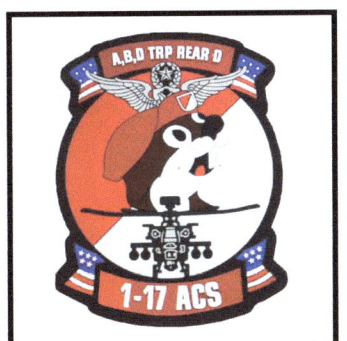

A Troop 1-17 CAV "ROUGHNECKS"

B Troop 1-17 CAV "BLACKJACK / BOOTLEG"

C Troop 1-17 CAV "CRUSADER / CRAZYHORSE"

C Troop continued...

 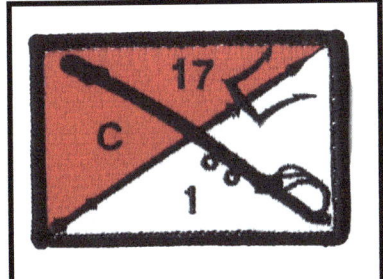

D Troop 1-17 CAV "DARKHORSE" / "DARK ANGELS"

E Troop 1-17 CAV "EXECUTIONER" / OUTLAW"

F Troop 1-17 CAV "BLACKHORSE" / "FOX"

HHT 1-17 CAV "WARHORSE"

Stetson Troop 1-17 CAV

2nd Squadron 17th Cavalry "OUT FRONT"

101st Airborne Division (Air Assault) Fort Campbell, KY (OH-58D) OIF 05-07, OEF 09, (AH-64) OIR 17-18

2-17 CAV Squadron patches

A Troop 2-17 CAV "ANNIHILATORS"

B Troop 2-17 CAV "BANSHEE"

B Troop continued...

C Troop 2-17 CAV "CONDORS"

C Troop continued...

D Troop 2-17 CAV "DIRTY DELTA" / "MUSTANGS"

D Troop continued...

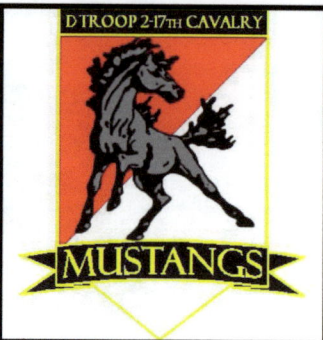

F Troop 2-17 CAV "COMANCHERO"

G Troop 2-17 CAV "LUCKY STRIKE"

3rd Squadron 17th Cavalry "LIGHTHORSE"

3rd Infantry Division, Fort Stewart, GA (OH-58D) OIF 07-08, OEF 09-10, OEF 12-13 (AH-64) OFS 15-16

3-17 CAV Squadron Patches

A Troop 3-17 CAV "SILVER SPURS"

B TRP 3-17 CAV "BLACKJACK"

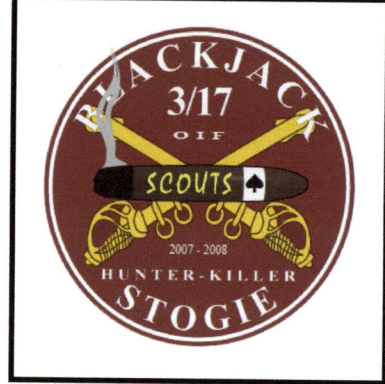

C Troop 3-17 CAV "CRAZYHORSE"

D Troop 3-17 CAV "BLUE TIGERS"

   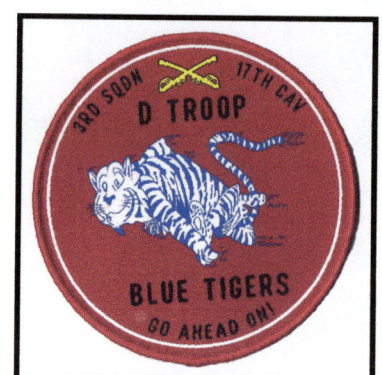

E Troop 3-17 CAV "SABERS" / "ENFORCERS"

F Troop 3-17 CAV "CENTAURS"

HHT 3-17 CAV "REDHORSE"

Why isn't there a 4-17 CAV when there is a 5, 6 and 7-17 CAV and why does the Army change unit names?

You may have noticed that there is a theme throughout this book. Aviation units particularly Air Cavalry units throughout history keep changing regimental affiliation and troop names. You might be asking why does this happen? Well, there is a regulation for that. Army Regulation 220-5, Designation, Classification and Change in Status of Units covers all the necessary steps to re-name and remove units from the active rolls.

Paragraph 2–3, Constitution, activation, designation, inactivation, and disbandment of Modification Table of Organization and Equipment (MTOE) units explains:
a. An MTOE unit must be constituted on the official rolls of the Army by the Chief of Military History.
b. A unit, once constituted, is eligible for activation. It is activated when transferred from the inactive to the active rolls of the Army. An activated unit is organized (brought into physical existence) by assigning to it personnel and equipment. A unit may be active but unfilled (that is, without personnel and/or equipment).
c. Ordinarily the designation of a unit selected for activation will be that of an inactive organization of the appropriate type that has the most noteworthy history.

For the purposes of our discussion here, subparagraph c is most important. The "unit that has the most noteworthy history". While the title of 'most noteworthy could be up for debate, it generally is fiarly easy to decide, but it does cause confusion and in the author's opinion degrades and devalues unit morale when somehting a group of people have worked are strived towards (often for years) is suddlenly thrown in the dust bin, because another name is "more noteworthy".

So, what happened to 4-17 CAV?

What happened with 4th Squadron 17th Cavalry is the same thing that has happened to many other units described in this book, as units were added or removed from the Army active rolls the Chief of Military History sought to keep the most historically relevant units active. This in the age of military downsizing has led to mayhem and also inadvertently led to a loss of unit identity is some places with constantly changing names and the loss of affected unit histories. After doing some research into unit histories, you will see below what happened to 4-17 CAV and how the elements that made that Squadron eventually formed what is now known as 4-6 CAV.

To learn how we got 4-17 CAV we first need to learn about Task Force 118. In 1987 in order to protect US flagged oil tankers during the Iran-Iraq war the US military began Operation Prime Chance. As a part of this operation AH/MH-6 "Little Birds" from the 160th Special Operations Aviation Regiment were used. As Prime Chance continued, it was felt that this mission was tying up this military asset so in January of 1988 Task Force 118 which featured the first use of armed OH-58D helicopters arrived in theater to take over for the "Little Bird" assets and free them up for other contingency missions. By the 1990's Task Force 118 had been reflagged as the 4th Squadron 17th Cavalry. On 10 January 1994, the 4th Squadron 17th Cavalry was inactivated and reflagged as the 4th Squadron 2nd ACR. Which then according to some sources became the 4th Squadron 6th Cavalry at FT Lewis, WA in 2004. According to others the remnants of Longknife Squadron of the 3rd ACR became 4-6 CAV around the same time. 4-6 CAV now refers to themselves as "REDCATCHERS" which was the old motto of 4-2 ACR. Confused yet? It is no wonder that units don't retain old designations when they are moved or inactivated then brought back later, because nobody can figure out anything other than the regimental lineage, which apparently is the way the Army wants it.

Why is There No Consistency with Company/Troop Names?

Companies or Troops in the Army are usually commanded by Captains (O3) and their names are for the most part usually related to the letter assigned them. Each Battalion or Squadron will have a certain number of companies or troops assigned to them. These units are designated with a letter of the alphabet starting with "A" and then "B" and so on. The only exception to this is HHC or HHT which stands for Headquarters and Headquarters Company or Headquarters and Headquarters Troop which is the company that the BN/SQN commander and his/her staff are assigned to for administrative purposes. Many times, an Alpha Troop will be named something beginning with the letter "A" for example, "Avengers". These names however are not controlled by any entity outside the unit which accounts for the ever changing and evolving nature of names and patches. In the past names have changed with a new commander because that person didn't care for the old name. One would hope for a sense of history to be applied and for example with B TRP 4-6 CAV being named "Black Death" it is, but this varies from unit to unit.

Patches from 4-17 CAV and 2nd ACR from prior to 9/11/2001

A Troop 4-17 CAV "WARRIOR" *A TRP 4-17 CAV "THUGS"* *B Troop 4-17 CAV "BLACK DEATH"* *C Troop 4-17 CAV "RENEGADES"*

N Troop 4/2 ACR "NIGHT THUG" *O Troop 4/2 ACR "BLACK DEATH"*

A grouping of patches from 4th Squadron 2nd ACR. From left to right; Subdued and Full Color Squadron patches, P Troop 4-2 CAV and Q Troop 4-2 CAV.

5th Squadron 17th Cavalry "OUT FRONT"

2nd Infantry Division (AH-64E) Camp Humphries, Korea (REESTABLISHED 2022)

5-17 CAV Squadron Patches

A Troop 5-17 CAV "APOCALYPSE"

B Troop 5-17 CAV "PALEHORSE"

C Troop 5-17 CAV "LIGHTHORSE"

D Troop 5-17 CAV "DRAGOONS"

HHT 5-17 CAV "VALKYRIE"

6th Squadron 17th Cavalry "PALEHORSE"

25th Infantry Division (OH-58D) OIF 08-09 4th Infantry Division, FT Carson, CO (AH-64)

6-17 CAV Squadron Patches

  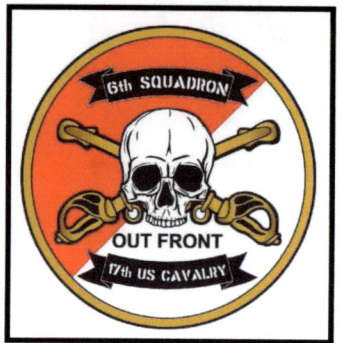 

A Troop 6-17 CAV "ACES"

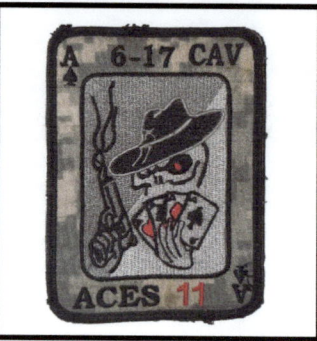
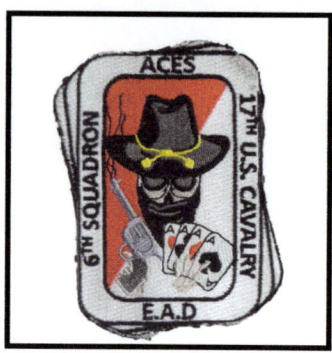

B Troop 6-17 CAV "BLACKFOOT"

C Troop 6-17 CAV "CRAZYHORSE"

D Troop 6-17 CAV "DAKOTA"

F Troop 6-17 CAV

G Troop 6-17 CAV "GRIZZLY

HHT 6-17 CAV "PALE HORSE"

7th Squadron 17th Cavalry "Palehorse"
101st Air Assault Division, FT Campbell, KY (OH-58D) OIF, OEF IX-XI, OEF XV,
(In 2015, 4-227th AVN was Re-Flagged as 7-17 CAV) 1st Cavalry Division, FT Hood, TX (AH-64)

7-17 CAV Squadron Patches

A Troop 7-17 CAV "AZRAEL" / "SHADOW" / "NIGHTMARE"

B Troop 7-17 CAV "BLACKJACK" / "SCALPHUNTER"

B Troop continued...

   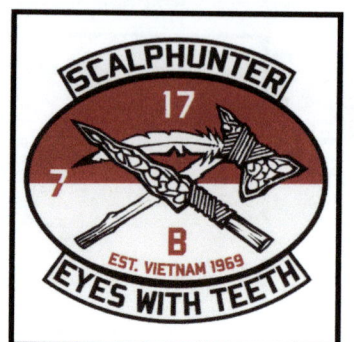 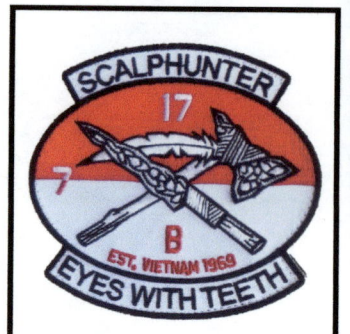

C Troop 7-17 CAV "CRAZYHORSE"

C Troop continued...

D Troop 7-17 CAV "WORKHORSE"

E Troop 7-17 CAV "IRON HORSE"　　　　　　　　　　　　　HHT 7-17 CAV "THOROUGHBRED"

NATIONAL GUARD and RESERVE UNITS

AH-64 A's from 1-149th AVN, TX ARNG (2004 photo by author)

7th Squadron 6th Cavalry "FAST GUNS"

US Army Reserve, Conroe, Texas (AH-64) OEF 06 (Unit inactivated and reflagged as 1-158th AVN in JUN 2008)

7-6 CAV Squadron Patches

A Troop 7-6 CAV "ASSASSINS"

B Troop 7-6 CAV "BONES"

C Troop 7-6 CAV "COYOTES"

C Company 1st Battalion 185th Aviation Regiment

MS ARNG, Tupelo MS (OH-58D/I)

C Company and HHC 1-185th AVN patches

In 1994, C Company 1-185th AVN's mission was changed to Armed Aerial Reconnanse and the unit was equpped with the OH-58D/I Kiowa Warrior. This lasted for a short time with the unit's aircraft eventaully ending up with 1-230th ACR of the TN ARNG.

1st Squadron 230th Cavalry "DESPERADOS"

Tennesse Army National Guard (OH-58D) OIF IX

1-230 CAV Squadron patches

A Troop 1-230 CAV "ASSASSINS"

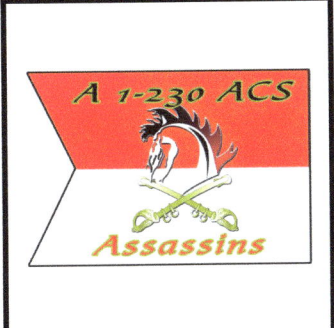   

B Troop 1-230 CAV "BLACKJACK"

C Troop 1-230th CAV "COPPERHEAD" / "COMANCHEROS"

D Troop 1-230th CAV "MOONSHINE"

E Troop 1-230 CAV "EXECUTIONER"

G Troop 1-230 CAV

4th Squadron 278th Armored Cavalry Regiment

Tennessee Army National Guard (AH-64) OEF VII

N Troop 4-278 CAV "NOMAD"

P Troop 4-278 CAV "PALADINS"

R Troop 4-278 CAV "ROUGUE"

S Troop 4-278 CAV

T Troop 4-278 CAV "WITCHDOCTORS"

HHT 4-278 CAV "HEADHUNTERS"

THE US ARMY AVIATION CENTER of EXCELLENCE (FORT RUCKER/NOVOSEL, AL)

AH-64E firing rockets at FT Rucker, AL (photo by author)

1st Battalion 14th Aviation Regiment "TOMAHAWKS"

Hanchey AAF, Fort Rucker / Novosel, AL (AH-64 D/E)

1st BN 14th Aviation Regiment Patches

A Company 1-14 AVN "FIREBIRDS"

C Company 1-14 AVN

D Company 1-14 AVN

HHC 1-14 AVN "WARHAWKS"

AH-64 Qualification Course, Class Patches

class patches continued...

    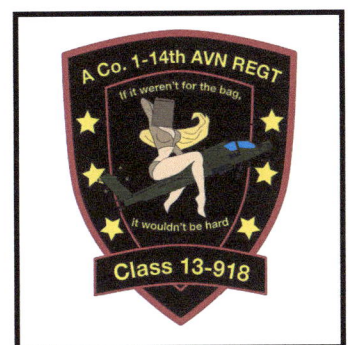

  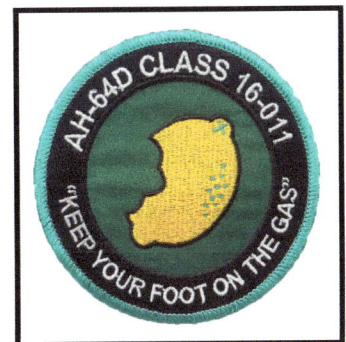  

class patches continued...

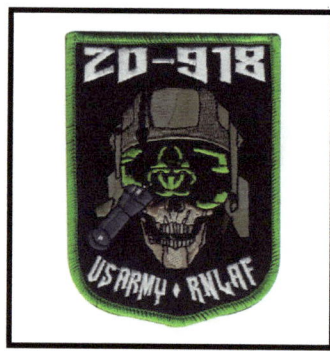

class patches continued...

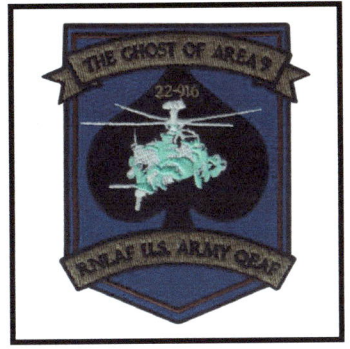

21st Cavalry Brigade "Continue the Attack"
Fort Hood, TX (AH-64 and OH-58D) 1985-2015

The 21st CAV BDE and Why It Should Be Remembered.

Every unit that has been featured in this book has participated in combat action during the War on Terror and all of its variously named missions except the 21st Cavalry Brigade. The reason I am including this brigade and its patch, is because without this brigade none of the units you have seen in this book would be what they are today.

Beginning in 1985 when it was known as the Apache Training Brigade (ATB) this unit was responsible for the collective aviation unit training for the United States Army. It trained every unit that fielded the
AH-64 A/D Apache and the OH-58D Kiowa Warrior helicopters. The trainers assigned to this unit touched every single one of the aviators that served in the units depicted in this book. If not directly then through second and third order effects form the aviators that the trained there. What Army Attack/Cavalry aviation is today is a direct result of their efforts.

Even though the Brigade was disbanded in 2015, the unit, its instructors and cadre left its mark on the units it trained and Army aviation in general.

AIRCRAFT SPECIFIC and GENERIC PATCHES

AH-64 APACHE Patches

OH-58D KIOWA WARRIOR Patches

more stuff...

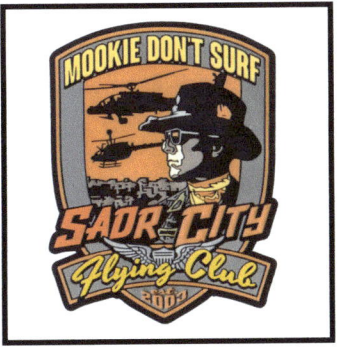    

ACKNOWLEDGEMENTS

There is no way that this book could have ever been made without the help of a lot of other people. Below is a list of some of the many folks who helped in getting me images or actual patches to be included in this project. Unfortunately some of these folks are no longer with us. This hobby will be poorer in their absence but we are all richer for having known them. Everything good in this book is because of these fine folks.

THANK YOU!

Aeroemblem, Keith Alan, Mike Anderson, Apache Warrior Foundation, Aviator Gear, Bomber Patches, Emil Balusek (RIP), David Barber, Freddie G Bee, Joe Belsha, Keith Benner, Dan Berriochoa, Rob Binz, Aubrey Bloom, Bomber Patches, Steve Boras, Perry Bowden, Jack Brink, Steve Bull, Brian Carbone, Billy Carroll, Clint Chamberland, Clint Cody, Kyle Connelly, Neil Covington, Dan Craytor, Jeff Crownover, Dan Cruz, Jay Decker, Chip Denton, Kevin Dishner, Chris Dixon, Tim Dolfka (RIP), Joshua Donaldson. Al Dupre, Rod Dwyer, Ryan Esterly, Tyler Finnigan, Daniel Flores, Bill Fox, Carl Fox, Jeremy W Gafford, Jake Gaston, Nate Graveman, Chris Greenhill, James Guffy, LTC Brian Haas, Joe Haberman, Alan Hahn, Nick Hatchel, Glen Hees, Jeff Hernandez, Mark Hough, Mary Elizabeth Izaguirre, Aaron Joe, Michael Jones, Eric Jurarez, Christopher Koth, Aaron Krupa, Billy L LeJeune, Jef Litvin, CW4 Matt Lourey (RIP), Tom Malnichuck, Tony Manfredi, Angelica Maria, Marco Martinez, John McDonald, Jim McLean, Herbert McTacops, Nick Miracle, Samuel Mo, Chris Morgan, Steve Myra, CV Nance, Ryan Nelson, Matthew Norbury, Jason North, Adonis Oldenburg III, Sean Onessimo, Mike Padgett, Carlos Par, Thomas Perrone, Brandon Provencher, Christopher Quill, Tanner Reed, Steve Reynolds, Lea A. Rhinehart, Ed Connell-Rhyah, Jason Richards, Angelo Rickert, Brad Ritzel, Tom Rude, Carlos San Nicolas, Alan Sanders, Steven Sandoval, Michael Sargent, Joshua William Sawyer, Bill Schlotzhauer, Chris Scoblic, Matt Silverman, Rocky Sudduth, Brian Serna, Dustin Smith, Keith Snyder, Steve Snyder, Jay Son, Rob Spara, Jennifer Cool Starmer, Shaun Steines, Andrew Stevens, Tad Stuart, LTC Andy Thaggard, Shaun Thurman, Shon Thompson, Kyle Thornton, Chris Tillman, Gabriel Torney, Kim Uher, US Company, Seth Vieux, Gary Watson, Andy Wilson, Jeff Wineland and Alan Woods

To submit corrections, make suggestions or inquires please contact the author at dngrpig@gmail.com

www.ingramcontent.com/pod-product-compliance
Lightning Source LLC
Chambersburg PA
CBHW041325290426
44109CB00004B/123